SURVIVING THE SENTENCE

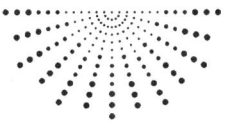

KIYA PAGE

Copyright © 2020 by Kiya Page

All rights reserved.

Published by Firebrand Publishing Atlanta, GA USA

No part of this book may be reproduced in any form or by any electronic or mechanical means, including information storage and retrieval systems, without written permission from the author, except for the use of brief quotations in a book review and certain other noncommercial uses permitted by copyright law.

For permission requests, write to the publisher, addressed "Attention: Permissions coordinator," at the email address: support@firebrandpublishing.com

Limit of Liability/Disclaimer of Warranty: While the publisher and author have used their best efforts in preparing this book, they make no representations or warranties with respect to the accuracy or completeness of the contents of this book and specifically disclaim any implied warranties of merchantability or fitness for a particular purpose. No warranty may be created or extended by sales representatives or written sales materials. The advice and strategies contained herein may not be suitable for your situation. You should consult with a professional where appropriate. Neither the publisher nor the author shall be liable for damages arising here from.

Firebrand Publishing publishes in a variety of print and electronic formats and by print-on-demand. For more information about Firebrand Publishing products, visit https://firebrandpublishing.com

ISBN: ISBN: 978-1-941907-29-0 (paperback)

ISBN: 978-1-941907-30-6 (ebook)

Printed in the United States of America

I dedicate this book to my daughter, my love, my heart, my soul and my motivation, De'Asia Page. Hold your head high baby!

Always remember from the womb to the tomb mommy got you. This book is also dedicated to all of the men, women and families who are Surviving The Sentence

CONTENTS

Never Would I Have Imagined ... ix

Chapter 1 ... 1
Chapter 2 ... 5
Chapter 3 ... 11
Chapter 4 ... 15
Chapter 5 ... 21
Chapter 6 ... 27
The Beginning of the End ... 33

About Kiya Page ... 45

NEVER WOULD I HAVE IMAGINED

Imagine lying in bed watching the news and a terrible story comes across your TV screen. I remember saying, "Wow, that is terrible what happened?". Then, to find out my child was suspected of committing the crime. Someone who I thought would never harm anyone. As a Mother, I was instantly worried. I began to pray. I said to myself, "This can't be true". I grabbed my keys and got into my car to go look for her. We had not talked in almost a month. Before I could find her, my phone rang.

It was her.

She was crying hysterically. I could sense that she was frightened. She began to tell me what her boyfriend had just done. He had just committed a murder and he made her drive the car. I asked, "Where are you?"

She gave me her location and I soon found her.

We talked. We cried. We talked more.

I tried convincing her that turning herself in was the best thing for her to do, and that I would be with her every step of the way. She was shaking and afraid. The only thing she would say was "Mom, turn myself in for what?"

I explained to her that she was on the news for what had happened. I told her I was pulling over to call the police. When I stopped the car, she jumped out and ran off.

CHAPTER ONE

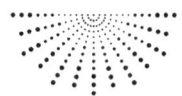

I was the mother of a three-year-old daughter when I gave birth to boy and girl twins in Marion, South Carolina. They were born on September 9, 1999 prematurely.

My son DeOnte, weighed one pound and was a breach birth baby. De'Asia my daughter, was two pounds and was delivered second by caesarian section. My son experienced some disabilities at birth and had to remain in the hospital a little longer than my daughter.

I was a nineteen-year-old mother of three children of whom I raised alone. I did have the support of family members. When I say alone, I mean that I was a single mother. My twins' father was incarcerated in the February following their birth. They were six months old, and I assumed the responsibility of raising them by myself.

Needless to say, it was hard. They both needed special care and so it was an issue with finding someone who would take care of their wellbeing while I pursued employment opportunities in an environment that wasn't very employment friendly.

I left South Carolina and moved to Greensboro, North Carolina to better myself for my family. Greensboro is where I had family, and they allowed me to come stay with them until I got on my feet. After living in Greensboro for ten years, I felt a need for change.

My children and I moved to Atlanta, Georgia. We loved Atlanta. My children were all getting older at this point. They began to find themselves and began making friends in the neighborhood and school. They were doing the normal things that children do. I found a job and a home that I was proud of. I was able to bring my grandmother to stay with me, and that was something I also took pride in. We were all in a good place and living our lives. I could not fathom the storm ahead.

CHAPTER TWO

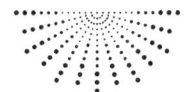

I can remember the first time they met. He was all she talked about, and she badly wanted me to meet him. She was excited and in Love... at least that is what she thought. I finally agreed to meet him. My other children had already told me a little about the guy and I had also heard my daughter speaking on things that she went through with him.

As soon as I met him, I knew something wasn't right. A mother's intuition kicked in. I said to my daughter, "I don't know about this guy. Something about him just did not sit right with me." She said, "Aw mom' you just gotta' get to know him".

Of course, she continued to see him by any means and against my advising her not to. As parents, we want what's best for our children. The more I talked to her, the more she rebelled. I remember someone telling me, the more I tried to keep her away from him the more it would only push her towards him. It was fracturing our relationship.

I took a step back and began to see things unfold. As a parent, I wanted her to learn from her mistakes. I never thought it would get to this point. She was sneaking out of the house, running away from home for days at a time, and missing days from work. Some days she would tell me that she had to work but really didn't. She would go to be with him.

We disagreed on how she handled her finances. I knew she was giving him her money. She would get paid from work and not have any money the next day. She admitted that she was giving her money to him, and when I asked about it, she became more rebellious. My daughter felt that she was in love. She had allowed a guy to manipulate her and there was no telling her any differently.

As a mother, I was overprotective. I tried to control where she went and how long she stayed out. I felt the crowd she was around was taking advantage of her. I was defensive because I raised my family to be a certain way and I expected them to reflect how I raised them. At that point, I felt I couldn't tell her anything. She went from working two jobs to staying out all night. She wouldn't tell me who she was with or where she was going

I felt I had done everything in my power to steer my children the right way. I was exhausted trying to reach her. I couldn't sleep. I couldn't think. I blamed myself. I questioned myself. Where did I go wrong as a parent?

When incidents like this happen, the focus is often shifted to the child's parents and upbringing. I had to realize I had done everything I knew to do as a mother. Still, as her mother, I could not just turn my back on her. I was basically all she had. I sought counseling and everything else that I felt was in the best interest of my daughter.

Before the situation I tried to seek counseling to mend our relationship. I felt the counselling was working. While looking at the news and seeing her face in connection with a crime, I thought about how I tried to keep her away from him. She was now on the run and facing felony charges. She was indicted for murder, felony murder, armed robbery, hijacking a motor vehicle and aggravated assault.

I didn't know where she was, and I hadn't heard from her. I watched the news in despair every time it was on, holding my breath and praying that nothing had happened to her. I didn't know if my daughter was safe or not. I just kept asking how could this happen? Why did this happen? I was hurt and very remorseful for the victim's family.

The next morning the news came on saying that my daughter had turned herself in. A feeling of relief overpowered me because I knew that she was safe and not running the streets.

CHAPTER THREE

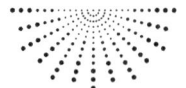

Kiyonna my oldest child, was supportive of her younger sister. She had embraced the big sister role for all of her siblings. She helped out around the house with cleaning, preparing meals, school clothes and homework. When they got older, I was able to leave Kiyonna in charge of watching over them while I ran errands or stepped away to have a moment to myself.

She never shied away from the big sister role. She stepped up more to help me support De'Asia while she was in the county jail.

She wrote to her and accepted her phone calls. She also visited and sent pictures.

Vantese the baby girl, was more upset with De'Asia, the situation she was in, and the situation that she had put us all in. My children faced ridicule at school and on their jobs. Vantese had expressed to me that she felt her sister had put me through unnecessary bullshit when all she had to do was listen.

Their relationship had always been strained, because they were so close in age they shared a sibling rivalry. This situation just compounded it. People pointed fingers and said terrible things to my children that put them on the defensive. They were saying things to my children like, 'oh your sister is crazy' or 'your sister is a murderer'.

They seemed to have their backs against a wall and were forced to speak out in defense of their sister, against complete strangers who had already judged and convicted De'Asia.

I felt helpless because I had already accepted the fact that it was something we would all have to go through. Although I know Vantese loves her sister, it's all frustrating for her. They do not speak like I would like them to, but I made the decision to give Vantese space and allow her to deal with this in the way she needs to. My hope is with time and age she will forgive her sister and they can build a stronger relationship.

De'Asia's twin brother, DeOnte, does not fully understand the situation. He was born breached and diagnosed with cerebral palsy. DeOnte and De'Asia are very close. They have an internal feel for each other. He knew his sister was in some kind of trouble. When he'd ask, I would try to explain to him that she could not come home for a while.

I told him that he could talk and visit her because he can't call her. My twins always seemed to feel for each other. On most days in the beginning, he would feel down. He was always an intense listener so he picked up on conversations that I would have about De'Asia. When we were alone, he'd ask about her every time the chance presented itself. All I could tell him was that she would be fine.

CHAPTER FOUR

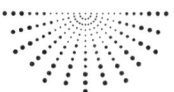

Three days after De'Asia turned herself in, it was time for her first court appearance. Before we arrived at the courthouse, we found out that her boyfriend had been arrested and charged with the same charges. This was definitely a high profile case.

My family and I arrived, and were instantly overwhelmed by the amount of people that were in attendance. News reporters approached us from every angle asking for a statement on behalf of my daughter. We did not make a statement. I sat in the courtroom, still in denial. I could not wrap my mind around the charges my child was having to face. I was stuck in a nightmare and I could not wake up.

The courts had appointed her an attorney, and she introduced herself to me in the courtroom. She seemed apologetic about the position I was in and also informative about my daughter's predicament. The attorney asked the courts that her first appearance be continued. I still had not gotten the chance to see or speak to my daughter. A request for bond was denied by the judge. I remember being worried as I left the courtroom.

I didn't know what was going on, or what was going to happen. I felt confused and helpless. I didn't understand how the court system worked. I was in the dark. Daily, I found myself wondering how this could happen to my family.

As my children searched my face for answers, I questioned myself. Did I really want to know how and why? I just wanted an easy answer. One week after she was detained in the county jail, I was able to visit her. Walking through those doors, the first thing I noticed was how dirty it was. I thought, *eww, how are they permitted to keep humans in this place?*

I sat down, afraid to touch anything while they called her for her visit. My heart sank when she appeared through the door being escorted by an officer. The jumpsuit she wore was dirty, and I was not used to seeing her that way. I asked her why her jumpsuit was dirty? She began crying. When she finally responded she said, "This place is dirty and nasty. I don't want to be here". She said she had asked for another jumpsuit, and they had ignored her.

My protective instinct pushed me to the nearest officer. I asked for whoever was in charge of the jail. When the lady came out, I asked why my daughter had on a dirty jumpsuit. They swore that they weren't aware of her needing a jumpsuit change. They immediately took my daughter out of the room and she returned with a cleaner jumpsuit. We continued our visit.

I could see in her face how afraid and hurt she was. I knew she could see how afraid I was for her. She could see how hurt I was, as well. Yet I was happy at the same time because I was actually able to see my child. The visit went horribly.

Neither of us could really talk because we were both crying. All she could say was "Mom, I didn't do it... I didn't do it." As her mother, all I could say to her was we would get through it together.

Visitation was only for thirty minutes once a week. I returned there every week, and every week was a different feeling. I'd base my conversation off of her vibe because I never knew how each visit would go. Of course she had her days so some visits were better than others. Sometimes she'd break down and sometimes we'd have good talks.

I was living the experience through her. Sometimes, she would break down because of the weight of what she was facing. Other times, we would have a nice visit and speak on good things. She'd tell me what was going on inside the jail and how officers treated them, and fights between inmates.

I warned her to stay away from trouble and that people around her weren't her friends. I guess it would be hard to do when you're in a room with 6 to 8 other females. She could call whenever she wanted to and she would call daily. Even though we talked on the phone all the time, we were both happy to see each other on Thursdays.

Sometimes I would go and be speechless. All kinds of memories would come back. From me going into labor with her and holding her as a baby, to the last time she was with the family. De'Asia was enrolled in a modeling school in Georgia and working two jobs. She had just gotten her driver's permit. I never thought this was where she would be at the age of 18.

A pit was carved out of the inside of me. I'd sit across from her on visits and feel empty. All I could think about was, what was my daughter not telling me, because I felt that she was still trying to defend him.

CHAPTER FIVE

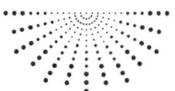

On Christmas Eve 2017, my child turned herself into the police. Our lives were forever changed. She sat in the county jail, for approximately two years. I visited every week. It never got any easier to see my child inside a jail. I couldn't explain the feelings I had, and I felt there was no one who understood.

I still cannot explain the feelings that I have. I was in a dark place yet still trying to hold it together for her and the rest of my family. I was a shell of myself. I would go through the everyday motions without a real focus. I'd sit at night and not remember anything that I'd done during the day. There was a time when I went to shower and realized once I had gotten in that I was still fully dressed. I was appreciative of everyone who had tried to offer their encouragement and support, but it never lasted for long in my mind and heart. I questioned God over and over. The only person that I would truly lean on was my daughter's attorney, because she was the only one with access to my child.

I felt I had established a relationship with her lawyer. She would call me to inform me of any court proceedings and to let me know whenever she'd heard from my child. I found myself leaning on her more often than not, because I didn't understand the system or what my daughter was going through inside the county jail.

She'd tell me over and over that things would be okay and encourage me to be strong. I felt she had my daughter's best interest in mind. De'Asia's father was living in North Carolina. We would conference call with her attorney to discuss her situation. Her father had experience with the court system and would voice how he was uncomfortable with the scenarios the attorney presented. I trusted him but we had no easy answers for the situation we were in. I just wanted it all to be over with.

My daughters boyfriend's trial began and it was not as easy to handle as I thought. For me, it was actually one of the worst parts since she had been arrested. The way they had my daughter on the stand and the questions they asked over and over. They attempted to make it seem as if she was an awful person. They put the blame on her for things she didn't do.

I wanted to scream at them from my seat. I wanted to speak up for my child but I had to sit quietly. Several times I was overwhelmed, and I had to get up and walk out of the courtroom. My child could not defend herself. I wanted to get up and defend her. The trial went on for about twelve days, and the jury took about five days to deliberate.

They returned with a verdict of guilty on all charges for him.

De'Asia entered a plea for 15 to 20 years. When they were ready to sentence her, I received a call from her attorney saying I had two hours to get to the courthouse. I still did not know a lot about the process but I found the break from a regular court date and the short notice for her sentencing hearing very strange. I was not able to stabilize any family support on such short notice. Things were extremely uncomfortable. I believe I began to panic. I was nervous for my child and nervous for trusting in her attorney.

We had convinced De'Asia that this plea deal was the best offer she could get. She still balked at pleading guilty to things she hadn't done but it was part of what she had to do. At Least that is how it was explained to me. So, that was what I thought as it pertained to her best interest.

At her plea hearing, I was permitted to address the sentencing judge. I was able to hold myself together long enough to get out what I wanted to say. All I wanted to say to the judge was that when you sentence my daughter you are also sentencing me because that's my child and I still have to be there for her.

I don't think it had any effect on the outcome, I just knew I had to say something on behalf of my daughter. The judge ignored her plea deal and gave her more time than was initially offered in her plea.

I felt faint.

I felt my breaths become short. Everything was spinning. I could not stand as tears began to fall from my face. I ran out of the courtroom.

CHAPTER SIX

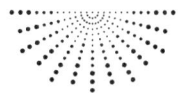

As told by Dallas McBride De'Asia's father

I failed her... That's the thought I have to live with when I process the reality. As a man, my belief is that most things concerning children are often centered around the man. The father. Even in his absence, a great father will always find a way to make his presence felt in a child's life.

He is supposed to guide, nurture, teach, protect, and provide, and the woman reflects that light.

She was a child... She was my child. And although I wasn't what I could be, I was the best father I could be, given my circumstances.

I should have been more.

I was 20 years old when the twins were born. I was sentenced to 103 months in prison when she was seven months old.

While I served my time, her mother went about making a better life for herself and her children. We lost contact for some time. I was able to reconnect with her years later. We had both grown up into our responsibilities and were able to establish a steady line of communication.

My daughter was eight years old at the time. We began speaking over the phone. Her mother and I explained my situation to her. She had questions she would ask, as she tried understanding what it meant to be in prison. I told her how I looked forward to seeing her and she responded the same.

She smiled a lot. She was bashful yet very well spoken for her age. Her mother had done a great job rearing her and her siblings. When the time came for a visit we were both excited and looking forward to it. However, when I walked out of the building towards her, she shied behind her mother and cried. I joked with her a lot about that time when she was eight. As time passed she shared with me that it was the shock of the officers, the prison fences, and her not knowing what to expect. She thought only bad people went to jail.

I understood.

When I got released, I went about making a way for myself and my children. Her mother and I lived in different states and shared custody of them. I was always careful of what I allowed her to see. She was sheltered to say the least.

We grew so close so quickly. She looked just like me. I would see her staring at me all the time. When I would ask her why she was staring, she'd just smile and say she didn't know. It was easy to tell she loved her father. She revelled in the attention she was given. She was spoiled by it, and I feel that's how it should be.

As children grow up though, you can't help but think they can recall certain instances and begin to put one and two together. Her questions became more pointed as her curiosity increased. When it was things that I was not ready to explain, I'd say to her that she would understand them when she got older. I never wanted her to grow up too fast and that was contrary to the times. I loathe the day when she first got her woman cycle and the day she became curious about boys.

I was in the county jail in the state of North Carolina when my relationship with my daughter began to get tumultuous. She was a teenager. She was disappointed and upset with my being locked up. She did not understand why I would risk leaving her and her brother again. I received letters from her venting her frustrations.

I would write back but I had difficulties explaining a lot of things. I was definitely offended by her questions and statememts a few times but, I understood her. I still had to be a father and exercise any method I could to reach her.

Her mother let me know that she was at a point where she was rebelling more and more. It was once said that a woman is often attracted to the kind of father figure she has in her life. I believe that to be true on certain levels. I came into my daughter's life when she was eight years old and swept her off of her feet with a father's adoration and love. I am aware of the many things she heard about me as well as some of the things she may have seen.

So, if she used those things and inadvertently painted an image of an ideal man, and that happened to be what she was attracted to... Just a thought. Maybe those misguided ideas played a role in the guy she chose to love. And if that is even a small part of what's true, then I failed my child.

De'Asia, my princess, I cannot take the blame for all the things you have faced in your young life. Neither can I prevent all the things you will have to face in your future. I want to apologize for not being better for you. I will continue to work on myself and be a better father to you. We have to live for each other. All of us. And we will. I am proud of your growth, young lady. It doesn't matter if we are agreeing or disagreeing on an issue, I will always walk with you.

I love you.

THE BEGINNING OF THE END

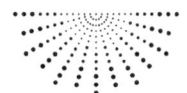

As Told By De'Asia Page

"Count time ladies. Lights On. Everybody on your feet," the officers yell. I sit up on my bunk and check the time on my tablet.

5:13 a.m.

My eyes close again as I lay back but not for long. I am startled by the officer banging on my cell door.

I jump up.

"Something wrong with your feet, Page?" she asks. All I can do is roll my eyes as I jump off of my bunk. The top bunk in a three woman cell. I stare as the officers walk off continuing to yell throughout the dorm. After they get their count, they yell for us to stand by our doors for breakfast.

I go to the sink and begin the morning routine of brushing my teeth. Then, I sit down to put my sneakers on. There is only a small amount of time before breakfast is called. I grab my coat to put over the sweater I am wearing just as someone yells out, "breakfast".

I push the button on my room wall to get the officers to unlock my door and I walk out of my building and head for the mess hall. I nod my head to speak to a couple of people I knew as we passed each other.

"Bitch, I told you I want my one hoe," someone behind me yells. I quickly turn around thinking she's talking to me, but she runs past me and hits the girl in front of me with a lock that she had put in her sock. A crowd forms around the fight. The lock in a sock is one of a number of weapons inmates use to exact punishment. I think to myself, "No wonder they don't give us razors."

After a cold breakfast, I walk back to my dorm and start cleaning my room. This is the same routine every day. We have to have our sleeping areas ready for inspection by 8 a.m. That means our lockers and footlockers have to be organized a certain way. Our ID's have to be on the left hand side of our uniform shirt, and our hair can't be on our shirt collars. It has to be up.

Once I am done cleaning my room, I go into the dayroom and begin sweeping. Some officers won't let us go to wellness unless they see us participating in dormitory cleanup. Wellness is the recreation time that we have every week. During the weekdays if we have an appointment we have to sign out and depending on who's on shift, we're not even getting out the gate without showing them our pass telling them where we're going.

While I was in county jail, I heard so many stories about prison. Although I'm still incarcerated, there is more freedom in prison, than being confined in the county jail.

The two years I spent in county jail couldn't have prepared me for prison. I quickly realized that prison was not the place to be friendly. You can't be friends with everyone. Being in prison is like a sea full of sharks who will smile in your face and prey on you and stab you in the back.

You meet a few real people, but most of these bitches will be your friend for what you can do for them. Living in such close quarters with 97 other females is beyond psycho to me. Definitely an adjustment. Watching the way we interact with each other is like watching female cheetahs protecting their babies.

I have learned that you cannot come into prison pretending to be someone you're not. My number one rule was to be true to myself no matter what happens. I knew that I would grow mentally and that my appearance would change, I'll change but I don't want prison to change who I am. I realized once you leave your mommy and daddy, nobody gives a fuck about you. Especially the system. You're basically another 10 digit number and a dollar in someone else's pocket.

I am grateful for my family's support. Still, I'm the one who has to hear the door slam. I'm the one being punished for the actions of other people.

I say this because I wasn't down with murder and now I'm in prison for 30 years of my life hearing these doors slam, all because he killed someone and I wasn't smart enough to listen to my mom.

I try not to think about the time I have to do but sometimes it gets hard. Especially when the people around you are going home. I am happy for them. I just wish it was me. Still, I understand and realize that when the man upstairs is ready for me, he will open these doors and no man will be able to stop me from walking out. That's faith. I have been locked up for four years. I feel like I have missed so much. I miss my first niece, my baby sister, older sister, and certainly my other half, DeOnte.

My mom tried everything in her power to keep me away from that boy. She even packed up and moved almost an hour away from him.

Did it work? No, because there are all types of public transportation. She couldn't protect and shield me from my boyfriend, and she can't protect and shield me now. Now is the time for me to grow up and live my life to the best of my ability behind these walls. Prison is a mental game and only the strong will survive. I don't have a choice but to accept what happened and move on.

I understand my love and loyalty for someone I was doing everything for, is what got me here. I accept that. Everything happens for a reason. I hate to say it, but I felt that me being in prison or me being dead were the only things that would keep me away from that boy. When he first met me he knew I was naïve and he knew he could manipulate me.

I thought he was my first love. If he didn't have anybody, he had me. I understand how loving him was dangerous mentally, emotionally, and physically. Even after the abuse started, I made myself believe that it was my fault. I made myself believe that if I didn't piss him off, he wouldn't hit me. I would have rather take the abuse than to see him leave me. He was my personal drug, and I was addicted.

I was jumping out of my bedroom window and sneaking out of my mom's house at 2/3 o'clock in the morning to go and see him. I'd make excuses for why I didn't show up to work. All I was doing was spending time with him because I felt that was more important.

I made excuses for the missed job opportunities when all along I was just with him. I'm finally realizing that the relationship I was in, was toxic. I'm finally understanding that he never belonged in my life. I accept responsibility for my actions but I feel he and his actions, got my life taken away from me.

Up until this very moment, I still made excuses for him. The same way I made excuses for the black eyes, busted lips, and for him cheating. I made excuses to the police the day I turned myself in for something he did. I lost friends and family in the process. I was trying to love him while gaining nothing but stress and depression. I made excuses for wanting to commit suicide over him. I even made excuses for why he did what he did the night we caught our charge.

I just want to say that I'm done making excuses for him or anyone else, most importantly, myself. I want to thank him for tearing me down because it is allowing me to build myself back up. The woman I am today is a force to be reckoned with, and as I move forward in life, I will do nothing but rise.

I caught my charge when I was eighteen years old. Today I am twenty. I've never been in trouble with the law, and I'm sentenced to 30 years in prison. This could have been avoided if I would have just listened to my mom. She told me my co-defendant was going to be my downfall, but me being young and having him all in my head, I was like, whatever, she's just saying that because she doesn't like him.

My mother was right.

When I caught these charges me and my mom weren't even on speaking terms because once again, I picked my man over the person that I knew loved and cared for me. But when I needed her she came running. When I turned myself in, and the police asked me who I wanted to call? I said no one.

I got locked up Christmas Eve of 2017. The worst Christmas gift I could have ever given my mother, right? When I got to jail, my mom had money on the phone and money on my book. That Thursday she was at visitation, and I hadn't even filled out visit forms yet.

My mom never missed a court date even though she had a job and three other children. The last time my mother hugged me was my birthday of 2017, because I was never at home. I wanted to be with him. I left home in the beginning of December because I wanted to be with my boyfriend, and that was the last time my mom saw me within arm's length of her.

It was also the last time she talked to me before I got locked up. In the last conversation my mom had with me she said, "I love you. You're 18 now, if you wanna run the streets and think you're grown go ahead, be safe."

Not listening to my mom got the rest of my life taken. I know my mom is living free, yet hurting because a part of her is locked up. Because of my actions, I am not home where I'm supposed to be.

My message to every young lady that may be in a similar situation, please listen to your mother. Coming in here walking through these gates, I was a young girl. Leaving out of these gates I will be a woman. WE ARE GOING TO BE OKAY MOMMY THIS IS ONLY THE BEGINNING TO THE END.

I LOVE YOU......

ABOUT KIYA PAGE

About me... I'm just a Jersey girl who always dreamed of being a successful entrepreneur. Just like many of us growing up in a single family home, I had real trials and tribulations.

As a child I made a lot of bad decisions. I had my first child at 16, then my twins at 19, then my baby at 23. I fought and fought to make sure my kids didn't see the things I saw and endured.

I worked tooth and nail at jobs that gave me pennies to provide for them. I had times when I was ready to give up and throw in the towel. But my God said no!! I'm not done with you. He turned my tears into a body armor that will protect me for years to come.

I moved to Atlanta with hopes of giving my kids a better opportunity, until one year ago my life and the lives of three other families changed for ever.

My armor was damaged once my daughter De'Asia made the wrong decision which gave me the inspiration to write this book. My goal for this book is to touch any and everyone who ever felt their life is meaningless because of taking the steps they took through life.

All I want to say is no matter what comes your way, always trust in God and then trust in yourself.

With that understanding you will Survive The Sentence.

www.ingramcontent.com/pod-product-compliance
Lightning Source LLC
Chambersburg PA
CBHW052125110526
44592CB00013B/1757